Athletes Who Made a Difference

SERENA WILLIAMS

Blake Hoena
illustrated by Sam LeDoyen

Graphic Universe™ • Minneapolis

Graphic Universe™
An imprint of Lerner Publishing Group, Inc.
241 First Avenue North
Minneapolis, MN 55401 USA

For reading levels and more information, look up this title at www.lernerbooks.com.

Main body text set in CCDaveGibbonsLower
Typeface provided by Comicraft

Photo Acknowledgments
The photos in this book are used with the permission of: Edwin Martinez/Wikimedia Commons, p. 28 (left); mirsasha/Flickr, p. 28 (right).

Library of Congress Cataloging-in-Publication Data

Names: Hoena, B. A., author. l Ledoyen, Sam, illustrator. l Graphic Universe (Firm)
Title: Serena Williams : athletes who made a difference / by Blake Hoena ; illustrated by Sam LeDoyen.
Other titles: Making a difference. Athletes who are changing the world.
Description: Minneapolis : Graphic Universe an imprint of Lerner Publishing Group, Inc., 2020. l Series: Athletes who made a difference l Includes bibliographical references and index. l Audience: Ages: 8–12 years l Audience: Grades: 4–6 l Summary: "Serena Williams has amazed tennis fans with her talent and spoken out against racism and sexism in the tennis world. She has also become a role model for a new generation of tennis players"— Provided by publisher.
Identifiers: LCCN 2019041851 (print) l LCCN 2019041852 (ebook) l ISBN 9781541578180 (Library Binding) l ISBN 9781728402963 (Paperback) l ISBN 9781541599451 (eBook)
Subjects: LCSH: Williams, Serena, 1981—-Juvenile literature. l African American women tennis players— Biography—Juvenile literature. l Women tennis players— United States—Biography—Juvenile literature. l African American women athletes—United States—Biography— Juvenile literature. l Working mothers. l Feminists.
Classification: LCC GV994.W55 H64 2020 (print) l LCC GV994.W55 (ebook) l DDC 796.342092 [B]— dc23

LC record available at https://lccn.loc.gov/2019041851
LC ebook record available at https://lccn.loc.gov/2019041852

Manufactured in the United States of America
1 – CG – 7/15/20

Table of Contents

CHAPTER 1

LEARNING TO PLAY

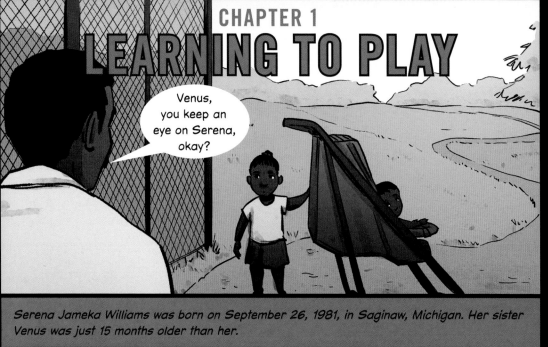

Serena Jameka Williams was born on September 26, 1981, in Saginaw, Michigan. Her sister Venus was just 15 months older than her.

Years earlier, Richard Williams had watched tennis pro Virginia Ruzici win the 1978 French Open. Since then, he had dreamed of teaching his daughters to play tennis.

He and their mother, Oracene Price, had already taught the sport to their daughters Yetunde, Isha, and Lyndrea.

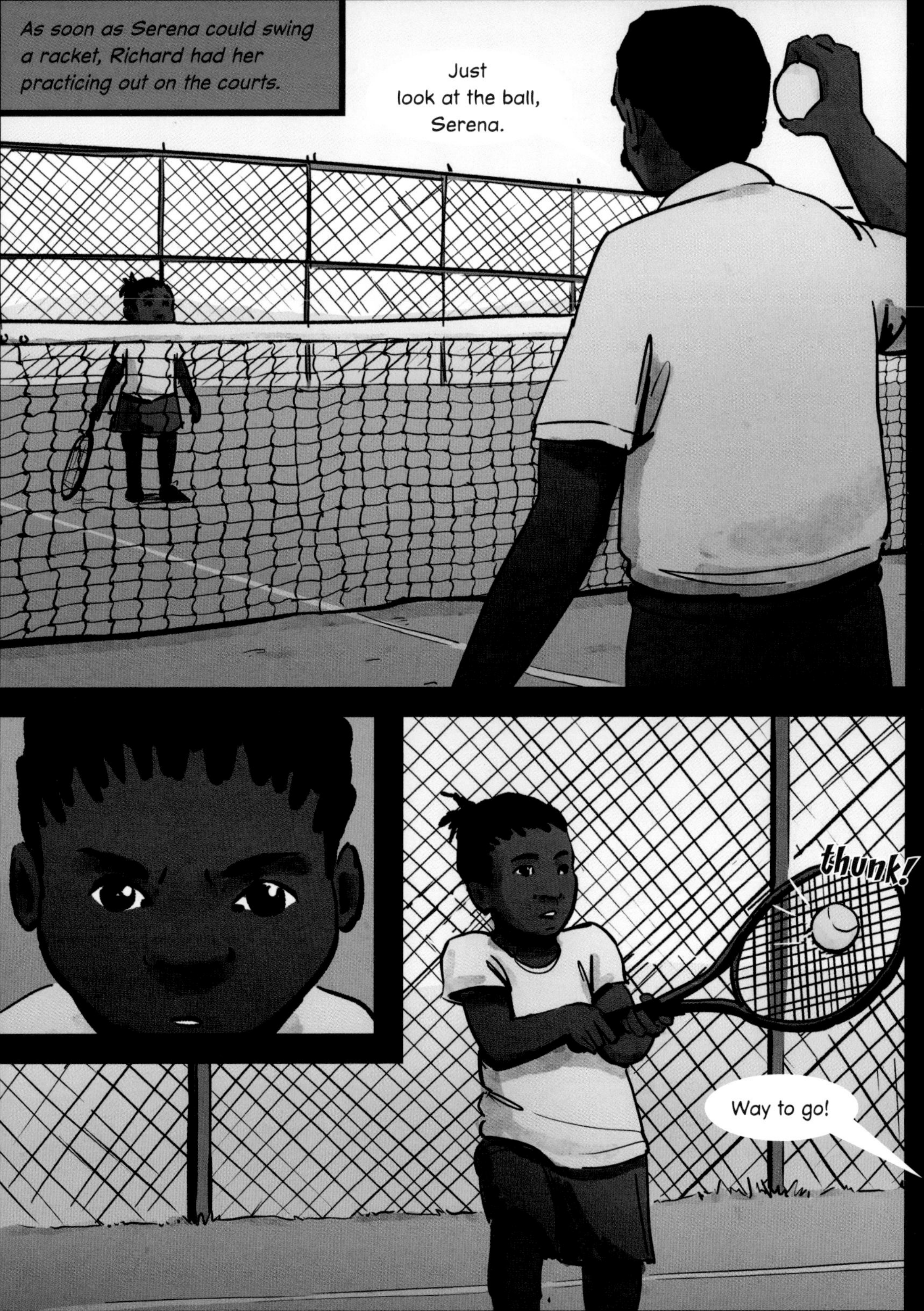
As soon as Serena could swing a racket, Richard had her practicing out on the courts.
Just look at the ball, Serena.
thunk!
Way to go!

Soon after Serena's birth, the Williamses had moved to Long Beach, California. Then in 1983, they had relocated to Compton, California. Housing there was more affordable than in Long Beach.

whack!

bang!

bang!

What was that?

Living in Compton allowed Richard to save money for his daughters' tennis equipment. But the area experienced high rates of crime and gun violence.

Okay, girls, practice is done for the day.

Still, the girls continued to train hard and improve their game. In 1989, Venus began competing in tournaments.

Go Venus!

I should be out there too.

. . . and Venus Williams wins the match!

I want to play in tournaments like V.

Not yet, Meeka. You're not ready.

Serena looked up to her big sister as a role model.

But later that year, Serena would join her older sister in competition.

If Venus can play in tournaments, so can I.

Meeka, I see you brought your racket today.

I might hit some balls with the younger kids between matches.

What her father did not know is that Serena had signed up for the tournament. She was planning to compete!

Great match, V!

Where's Serena?

I don't know where your sister is.

Mr. Williams?

Game, set, and match, Serena Williams.

whack!

Meeka, look at you. You won!

You aren't mad I entered the tournament?

Nah, I'm proud of you. Proud of both my girls.

That day, Serena and Venus both made it to the final match. It was the first time Serena would face her big sister in a tournament.

Venus was the victor. But Serena would play her again—many times.

CHAPTER 2

TRAINING IN FLORIDA

By 1991, Richard felt his girls needed to take the next step in their training.

Serena, Venus, this is Mr. Rick Macci. He runs a tennis camp in Florida.

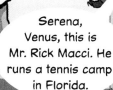

I invited him here to watch you practice tomorrow.

The next morning, Richard brought Macci to the courts where his daughters practiced.

Seeing the rough shape of the courts, Macci had his doubts. The girls were also unpolished in their play.

Not long after Macci's visit, Richard moved the family to Florida. There, Serena and Venus began to receive professional training at the Rick Macci Tennis Academy.

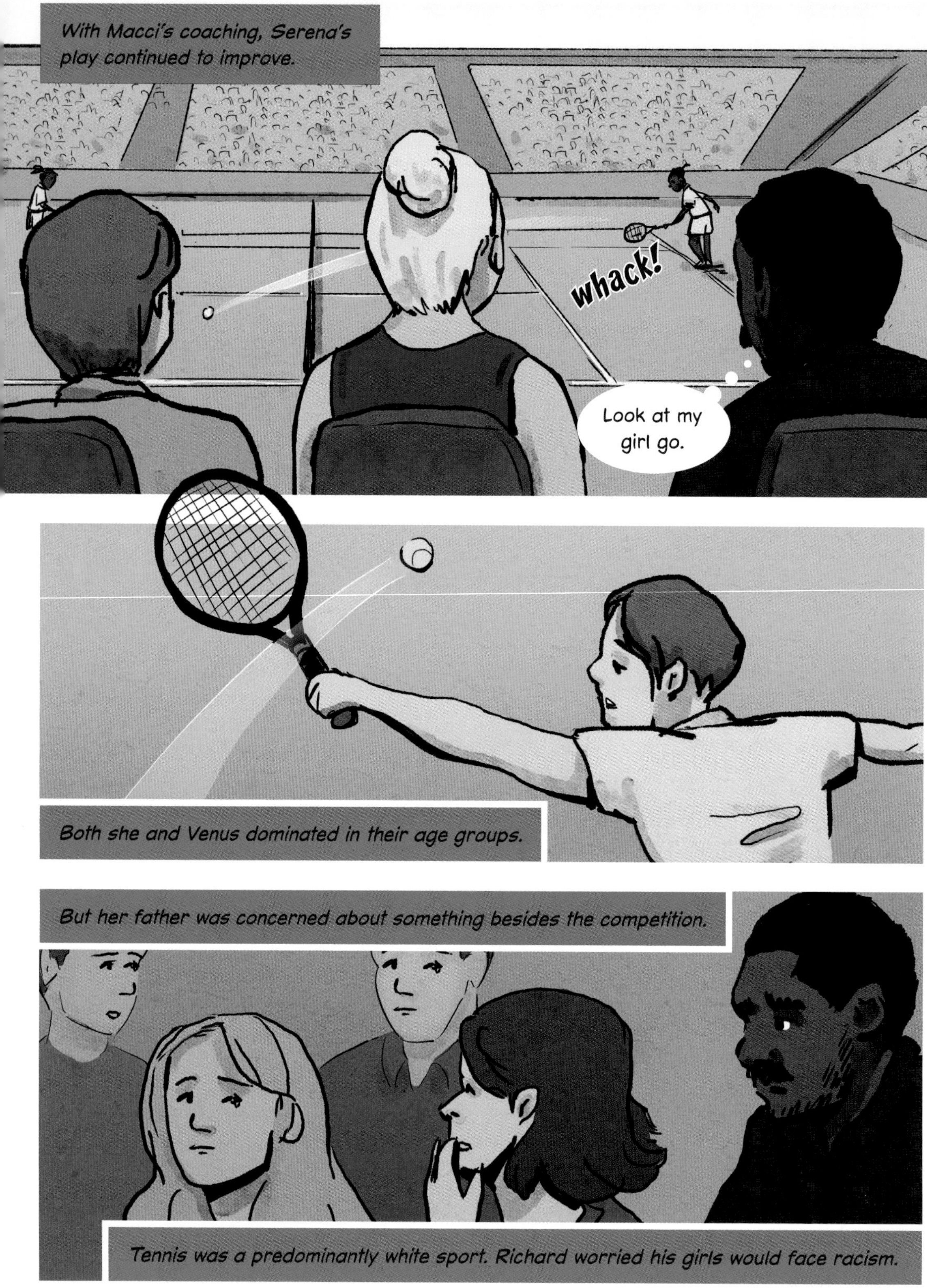
With Macci's coaching, Serena's play continued to improve.
whack!
Look at my girl go.
Both she and Venus dominated in their age groups.
But her father was concerned about something besides the competition.
Tennis was a predominantly white sport. Richard worried his girls would face racism.

He also did not want to put too much pressure on them to win.

I don't want them playing against each other, not yet. And maybe only a couple tournaments a year, if any.

That's going to limit their growth as athletes.

They're still just kids and need to have some fun.

Richard also wanted the girls to have time to focus on school.

Hey, Meeka.

Bonjour, papa!

What are you studying?

I'm learning French, because one day I'm gonna win the French Open.

But tennis was never far from Serena's mind.

CHAPTER 3

TURNING PRO

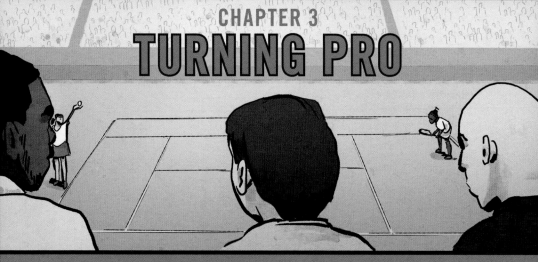

Venus turned pro in 1994. A year later, on October 28, 1995, Serena played her first professional match. She was only 14 years old. Her opponent, Annie Miller, was four years older.

whack!

THUNK!

Game, set, and match. Annie Miller, 6–1 6–1.

Serena lost that day. But two years later, she would start to make waves in tennis.

During the 1997 Ameritech Cup in Chicago, Illinois, sixteen-year-old Serena beat Mary Pierce. Pierce was ranked seventh best female tennis player in the world.

In the next round of the tournament, she beat Monica Seles, who ranked fourth in women's tennis.

Serena ended the year ranked as the 99th best female tennis player in the world.

Early in 1998, Serena met a familiar opponent during her first Grand Slam. She faced Venus in the second round of the Australian Open.

Serena played tough in the first set, losing 7–6 in a tiebreaker.

OUT!

The second set did not go as well for Serena. Again, she lost to her big sister.

Good match, Meeka.

You too, V!

But the following year, Serena would do something her big sister had not yet achieved.

In September 1999, Serena won her first Grand Slam. She beat Martina Hingis, who was ranked number one in the world, in the US Open final.

That same year, Serena began studying fashion design at the Art Institute of Fort Lauderdale.

Maybe I'll design my own tennis outfits one day.

While the Williams sisters played hard against each other, they also played well as a team. In 2000, they won gold medals in women's doubles at the Olympic Games in Sydney, Australia.

At the end of 2000, Serena was ranked sixth in the world.

At a 2001 tournament in Indian Wells, California, Serena was set to play Venus in the semifinal. But Venus had injured her knee earlier in the tournament.

I don't know if I can play.

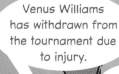

Venus Williams has withdrawn from the tournament due to injury.

Booo! Booo!

People were upset. Some thought Venus had faked the injury so that Serena could move on to the final match.

The day of the final match, fans were hostile as Venus and Richard took their seats.

BOOO! BOOO!

Some even shouted racial slurs.

The crowd's anger was also directed at Serena, who was still just a teenager at the time.

Amid the applause, there were boos whenever Serena scored a point.

Ace for Serena Williams!

clap! clap! clap!

Booo!

Serena managed to keep focused on her game and win the match.

clap! clap! clap!

BOOO! BOOO!

But the incident left her shaken. Serena felt threatened by the crowd's jeers and racial comments. Because of how spectators treated her, she would not play at Indian Wells again until years later.

CHAPTER 4
NUMBER ONE

In 2002, Serena faced her big sister again. This time it was in the final match of a Grand Slam, the French Open.

And this time, Serena won, beating Venus in straight sets, 7–5 6–3.

That victory began a winning stretch for Serena. She went on to beat Venus in the 2002 Wimbledon final, another Grand Slam.

The Wimbledon victory earned Serena the ranking of number one female player in the world.

She also beat her sister in the final match of the 2002 US Open.

WHUMP!

Serena became known for her strength and intensity.

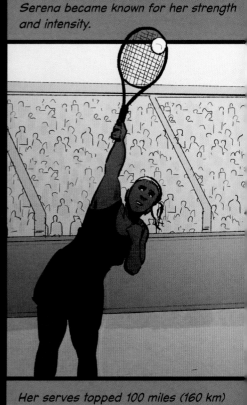

Her serves topped 100 miles (160 km) per hour!

In 2003, Serena and Venus made it to the final match of the Australian Open. Once again, Serena was victorious over her big sister.

She had just won four Grand Slams in a row, making her the most dominant player in tennis.

The next few years brought both triumphs and struggles for Serena. She won the 2003 Wimbledon final, her sixth Grand Slam victory.

WHACK!

But later that year, a knee injury kept her off the court for months.

During her time away from tennis, Serena debuted her own clothing line called Aneres.

Recovered from her injury, Serena won the 2005 and 2007 Australian Opens. In 2008, she regained her number-one ranking.

While winning championships, Serena was also inspiring a new generation of tennis players.

Everyone's dream can come true if you stick to it and work hard.

Throughout her career, Serena worked to help underprivileged youth develop their game.

In 2015, Serena ended her boycott of the Indian Wells tournament. She felt nervous about her return. But she hoped her decision would be a positive influence on others.

Stepping onto the court was a powerful moment for Serena. She was met with cheers and applause from the crowd.

In January 2017, Serena won the Australian Open final while about eight weeks pregnant. On September 1, she and Alexis Ohanian had a daughter, Alexis Olympia Ohanian Jr.

The couple married that November.

After taking time off with her new family, Serena worked to get her game back. In the fall of 2018, she played her way into the US Open final against Japan's Naomi Osaka.

It was Naomi's first trip to a Grand Slam final. She outplayed Serena in the first set, winning 6–2.

OUT!

The second set started better for Serena. But then . . .

Code violation, coaching. Warning. Mrs. Williams.

The chair umpire thought Serena's coach was signaling to her. The rules of tennis don't allow players to receive coaching during a match.

I don't cheat to win. I'd rather lose.

The chair umpire gave Serena a warning for what he saw.

At one point in the second set, Serena was winning 3–1.

THWACK!

Game, Osaka.

But after making a mistake, she threw her racket down in anger.

Code violation, racket abuse. Point penalty. Mrs. Williams.

It is against the rules for a player to purposely break their racket during a match.

Serena was upset.

You stole a point from me.

Code violation, verbal abuse. Game penalty. Mrs. Williams.

With the game penalty, Osaka was now winning the set 5–3.

Serena had had enough. She felt the umpire's penalty was sexist.

There are men out here that do a lot worse. But because I'm a woman . . . you're gonna take this away from me? That is not right.

Serena seemed off her game after the last penalty. She lost the match to Osaka.

Game, set, and match. Osaka, 6–2 6–4.

Osaka became the first Japanese player to win a Grand Slam title.

At a press conference, Serena stood by her reactions at the US Open final.

I stood up for what I believed in. I stood up for what was right.

Other tennis stars spoke out in support of Serena's stance.

Serena started 2019 strong. At the Australian Open, she beat number-one ranked Simona Halep to make it to the quarterfinals. Serena continues to be a force on the courts.

AFTERWORD

During her career, Serena Williams became one of the most accomplished tennis players in history. She has won a total of 23 Grand Slam singles titles.

Serena changed the way female players approach the game. In recent times, more women use a hard-hitting style similar to hers. Serena also proved that anyone could play tennis, no matter what they looked like or where they grew up. As a result, many young African American women were inspired to become tennis stars like Serena.

ATHLETE SNAPSHOT

BIRTH NAME: Serena Jameka Williams

BORN: September 26, 1981, Saginaw, Michigan

Awards
of Note

- ◆ Grand Slams (singles)—23
- ◆ Grand Slams (doubles)—14
- ◆ Grand Slams (mixed)—2
- ◆ Olympic Medals (singles)—1 gold
- ◆ Olympic Medals (doubles)—3 gold
- ◆ Associated Press Female Athlete of the Year—
  2002, 2009, 2013, 2015, 2018
- ◆ ESPY Award for Best Female Athlete—2003,
  2013

SOURCE NOTES

5, 7, 9   Serena Williams, On the Line. New York: Grand Central
          Pub., 2009.

24–27   ESPN, "2018 US Open Highlights: Serena Williams' Dispute
          Overshadows Naomi Osaka's Final Win," YouTube video,
          14:40, September 8, 2018, https://www.youtube.com/
          watch?v=uiBrForlj-k.

27   US Open Tennis Championships, "2018 US Open
          Press Conference: Serena Williams," YouTube video,
          9:53, September 8, 2018, https://www.youtube.com/
          watch?v=2KIyoTEqrxo.

GLOSSARY

ace: a point scored by a serve that the opponent fails to return

game: a segment of a tennis competition. There are four points in a game.

Grand Slam: one of the four major tournaments in tennis. The Grand Slam tournaments include the Australian Open, the French Open, Wimbledon, and the US Open.

match: a segment of a tennis competition. A match is won by winning the majority of three or five sets.

racism: the belief that some races of people are better than others

set: a segment of a tennis competition. Typically, the first player to win six games wins the set.

sexist: characterized by sexism, or discrimination based on a person's sex

straight sets: a situation where a player wins all the sets in a match